# IN THE
# NIGHT
# WATCHES

Dr. Mary Ann Colarusso

Love bears all things,
believes all things,
hopes all things
endures all things
Love never fails

Helen Zwick

# IN THE NIGHT WATCHES

*Helen Zwick*

**TATE PUBLISHING**
AND ENTERPRISES, LLC

Published by Tate Publishing & Enterprises, LLC
127 E. Trade Center Terrace | Mustang, Oklahoma 73064 USA
1.888.361.9473 | www.tatepublishing.com

Tate Publishing is committed to excellence in the publishing industry. The company reflects the philosophy established by the founders, based on Psalm 68:11,
*"The Lord gave the word and great was the company of those who published it."*

Book design copyright © 2014 by Tate Publishing, LLC. All rights reserved.
*Cover design by Gian Philipp Rufin*
*Interior design by Manolito Bastasa*

Published in the United States of America

ISBN: 978-1-63268-208-6
Poetry / Subjects & Themes / Inspirational & Religious
14.07.01

To God Almighty,

# CONTENTS

## CHOICES

## FOCUS

## NATURE

## ETCETERA

# ACKNOWLEDGMENTS

Much thanks and love to my pastor, Kim Wilcox, who encouraged me to write these poems and to my husband, George, for his patience and willingness to help me with all the computer work. Love you much, George.

Many thanks and love to Madonna Sieber and Jeanette Barron for their prayers for this book and my life.

It is my pleasure to be a willing pen for the Lord. May he receive all of the glory.

# CHOICES

So many opportunities arise in a day. Seeking God first thing in the morning will give you direction. Please consider spending time with God. He is waiting to hear from you.

# BACKPACKS

Saw a sheep, yes, I did
He was wearing a backpack
Well, it threw him off balance
And into a tree he did fall

Another sheep came to him
No backpack wearer was he
For he was free
Said he to the first sheep
Drop that pack
And be free like me

Well, the first sheep
Thought and thought
What would I do without my pack?
Slowly, he started to
Remove his pack
And lo and behold
He straightened up
And moved lightly

Well, the moral of the story is
Let the Lord have your burdens
For you, sheep, weren't
Meant to bear them

# BIRTHING

It's true, this place,
This earth is the birthing place
For your kingdom O Lord
Or for the place of darkness
This is our choice
For you have given us that power
What kingdom will you choose this day,
The one of life or death continuously?

Lord, your kingdom is glorious and true
Where sin does not abound or live
Where love, truth, trust grows each day,
So we can walk in the way

Not of darkness and anguished cries
Where your love and truth are not, they sigh
The worm lives again and again to the tortuous cries
Of the children of darkness the ones who continually die

So chose this day and every day
Until you see the face of God
Welcoming you home from the birthing place
To live and not die

# CHECK UP

Each day, the Lord gives us grace upon grace
To us who do not deserve His favor or mercy
It is in the inner parts
That He wants to be clean and pure

To be real, no falseness to be found
So we can come before Him
And be His children

This is the day to check your heart
And your ways
For if you should meet Him today
Where will you stand?

# CHOICES

Choices are many to be made in this world
Life eternal is the most important
Do you not think?

Acceptance of our Lord
He is all that it's about
What would you give or sacrifice for one soul
Beloved or not

Would you give all you've
Known and loved
To save just one

Just so the angels may rejoice
But what of Jesus
Would this not be His supreme delight?

For you see, He does not want even one to perish
But for all to see the light

So what would you sacrifice
Or choose this night?

# INHERITANCE

Each one of us has an inheritance
Living and true
Eternal light or darkness
What's for you?

Jesus the Christ came to save
Such as us
For the coming world
Without sins' lusts

Bright as the morning sun
Is the Son of God
Welcoming you to His side
Will you be the one or hide?

Leave the world and its
Sins behind
What's needed is a
Change of heart and mind

So come one, come all,
To be His future bride
To live with Him
Side by side

# RELATIVES

God has decided
Before the world was made
That you would be His

A son or daughter not
A servant or a friend
But a blood relative
Through Jesus Christ
His own

Still, today, the decision
Is yours
A son or daughter of God
to be loved for all eternity
Or lost and forsaken forever

# RISEN

A bright new morning has arrived
With wonderments and promises to behold
New relationships, new experiences
For the Son of God has risen

Have you claimed Him for your Lord?
The One and Only
For He has risen from the grave
And has come to save you for all eternity

God the Father, Son and Spirit
To be with you as one
When you choose Jesus the Christ
As your Savior

# STRADDLING

Centuries ago, the Lord spoke
He made the world and all that is in it
He spoke again and His words have gone forth
Not to return empty but to fulfill His plan

It's great to belong to God
Who created us
But more so, 'cause He has a plan
For you and me

We may not understand
But neither did they, centuries ago
When He walked the earth
But, you can see now part of His plan
Salvation for all
For He does not want to lose one person

So consider which side of the fence you are on
Don't straddle it
Come to Jesus
Pick His side

# THE EYES OF GOD

The eyes of God
Are open and bright
There is no fear or shame

The eyes of God
Are loving and kind
But don't be lax
And think they are
Not just

For the eyes of God
Know you
When you were formed
And see you now

Look unto the eyes of God
For He is your Savior, Redeemer

He will welcome you
Into His kingdom
Or
He will look away

Look into the eyes of God
It's your choice
This day

# THE FEAST

Come, come,
To the feast of the Lord
Bring your bowl in one hand
And your plate in the other

Be filled with the Lord
Never again to thirst or be hungry
For that is not of the Lord

The Lord's feast
Is love, kindness, purpose, and strength
To fill your every need
With the Lord Jesus Christ

His ways for your life
His will is much higher than ours
Be filled with His Presence
Come to the feast of the Lord

# THE WIGGLES

Be still and know that I am God
We are told to do
But soon the wiggles
Start here and there

Your body may be silent
But, oh, the thoughts abound much
A little wiggle here
And a big wiggle there

Try to quiet your mind and
Listen for the small still voice
Much effort it might be
But, oh, to hear the voice of my Lord
Is worth it all

So say good-bye to the wiggles
Ask the Holy Spirit to train you
To stay and truly wait upon
The Lord

# TOMORROW, TOMORROW

No one is promised tomorrow or even today
So that we can go on our selfish way
Getting all the "toys" and money on life's path
Will not save one from the final death

The bright promise of Jesus Christ
Who died for each one of us
To live with Him forever more
Is the only promise that is real
And that, truly should be our zeal

So come one, come all
Ask Him into your life
Accept Him as Lord and Savior
So you, too, will become His wife

# VISION

The former and the latter rains will be complete
When Jesus the Christ is on His seat
No more strife, no more division
For God has completed His vision

Woe to those who chose Him not
For now they know they are on the spot
Never to be in heaven or at His side
Why, oh, why did they hide?

Choices were made
And lives were sealed
Now they have lost the power to be healed
Some time there still is
Your choice to be His

# 24/7

Talk, Talk, Talk
Radios, TVs, and computers
Are on
What fun! Games galore
iTunes, iPods, texting, Facebooks, and Twitters
Who listens to people anymore?

Most of all where is the fear of the Lord
Not this town or place
"I AM" of ancient days
Has been replaced by the
I am…self-sufficient individualist

Do you seek to know God's face?
Oh…all you want is His benefits
"God Bless, America"
But what of Him

He is the Father who gave His only begotten Son
Just for you!
So you wouldn't have to go to hell
Where the worm and torment never cease

Oh...excuse me
Hell's a party place you say
The darkness, deep pools of darkness, anguished cries of the
party goers
Smells of sulfur and flesh mingle

Soon a distant ruby light
Where Satan and his horde hold court
But no party goers there
Just the devils delight

Why, I cry, do you want to go there?
Just because your friends go
You still can escape

Look to the Lord
Cry out His name
Save me, Lord Jesus
Help me this night
Seek Him for He is the only way
To the Father this day

# FOCUS

Each day, you decide what will hold your attention. Once the decision is made, your day unfolds to be filled. Keeping your focus on the God who made you will strengthen you, and direct your path throughout the day, with much accomplishment and victory.

# ALL IN ALL

As it is written, so it shall be
As God has written in His word
Follow His commandments
And do His biding
Love your neighbor as yourself
For love never fails

Confess your sins to Him, and be really sorry
Not just lip service, but from your heart
Leave it with Him and move on
For the Lord God Almighty loves you

When in doubt about an action or situation,
Immediately, take it to Him in prayer
And wait for the answer not blundering
Into trouble

Keep your mind on the God who made you
Focus, focus, focus on Him,
And your path will be established

In all and all
Love the Lord God with all your heart
Soul and strength
And remember love never fails

# BABY OH BABY

Did you ever see a baby when they walk?
They amble to and fro
Then suddenly shoot straight for their desire
They know what they want!

Aren't we like that too?
We think we're on the path to God
But suddenly we, too, see the real place
We want to be
And leaving all behind, shoot straight to Christ

For without Him in our lives, we are not alive
We're just flesh in this world subject to its desires
When we search for Christ and find Him
Freedom and love reigns in our hearts
And Christ is alive in us

# DON'T

Don't give up
Don't give in
When sin is trying to get you

Keep your eyes on
The Lord God Almighty
Jesus Christ is His name

Cry out to the Holy Spirit of God
For help
Get fortified by Him

Keep your sight and heart
On the Lord
Don't give up
Don't give in

# FOCUS

The least is the greatest
And the greatest must fall
For when the Son of Man comes again
To judge the living and the dead
All that was recorded
Will be opened to all

Why will this come about?
Why must it be?
For it has been foretold centuries ago

So live each day as a servant to all
In love only, so you may not fall
And come to see Jesus
The Master of All
For love conquers everything great and small

Don't give up or in
To sin to abound
But keep your eyes on Jesus
The soon coming King

# LIES

Have you been listening to the lies?
You are not good enough, talented enough,
Pretty enough or rich enough
The devil's a pretty good liar

Stand on the truth
Jesus the Christ is His name
You are the righteousness in Christ
A child of the King

He has created you
And it is a very good thing
Special and different in His sight
For He came to save and redeem you
To live in His glorious light

# PRAISE

It is important to sing
Praises to the Lord
Mighty words that are fine and true
For he gives his children rest
So they may do their best

Praise the Lord no matter the time of day
As your praises rise, so do you
To keep your focus on God alone
For our God is worthy of praise

# QUACK, QUACK

Lord, I have all my
Ducks in a row
The bills are paid
And everyone is okay

Suddenly, my husband is sick
I'm not doing very well
The union's threatening strike

When did it happen?
How is the question?
For you see all my
Ducks are in a row.

I depended on myself and not you Lord
When did I slip and turn away
Will you come to me and stay?

Now my sight is on you, Lord
I'm looking for you in your word
I depend on you, Lord
For you see all my ducks were not in a row

# SEEMS LIKE

When you are in a situation
Where there seems to be no hope
Or boxed into troubles
That has no end

Don't give up!
Turn to Jesus Christ
He is the waymaker
The truth and life

He has the words of life
That brings hope and healing
To every situation or problem
There is none other like Him

For He has loved you
Before you were born
And has knitted you into His plan
Persist in seeking Him
Don't let anyone or anything stop you
Keep your eyes on Him!

# THE HAVES

Have you looked upon the Lord today?
Made him your focus the first thing upon awakening

Have you spoken to Him of your desires?
For the life walk of your day

Have you stopped and listened for Him
For His voice in all that is around you

Have you searched for Him in His Word for this day?

Have you told Him you love Him?
In each and every way

# TURNING

The seasons are turning
The fall has been spent
And soon winter will be upon us

The harvest is ripe in many places
Make sure of your standing with the Lord
Spend time with Him
So you will know His voice for sure

He will guide and protect you
And never let you down
What "seems" as a trial
Will be for His glory

Be encouraged by His word
Focus on Him
Not turning to the left or right
For the Lord God Almighty is our life and deliverer

# 11:59

Hold on!
Stand firm
Be alert
Don't let go
Keep your focus on Jesus

Even if it's 11:59
And disasters are at your door,
Don't retreat
Work through them with Jesus
He is the way, the truth, and the life

# NATURE

Nature is God's way for you to stop and experience his creation and know that he is God!

# SHELLS

Shells of all sizes are brought up by the sea
Plain white, different shades of color
Including black and gray
They are all God's creation
Each different but beautiful in His sight

Some are broken
Some are whole
Others have a chip or two
Just like God's children
Who He loves holy
Wholly like you

# SKY

Thank You, Lord, for the
Evening sky
Thank You, Lord, for the
Morning sky
And the skies in between

The shades of blue, white
Pink, gray, and even black too
Brings glory to you

For You are the greatest artisan
Some call you the greatest engineer
Some the greatest architect

For You created all
For your glory
You are God alone and
There is no other

# SPRING

Crocuses, daffodils, and
Tulips supreme
God's creations beautifying
And coloring the scene

A newness, a freshness
For nature and man
Just look around
To see God's plan.
For rebirth and a new life

Come to the Lord
For He is the Creator and
Keeper of all

# THE BEACH

The walkers walk the beach
Some play tag with the waves
Others plunge into the waves
To look for the treasures of the sea

When you read the word
Are you a walker, tagger,
Or do you plunge deep
To find the promises and treasures
For you to keep?

# THE OCEAN

The ocean declares God's glory
It brings pleasure to the eye and ear
It brings food for the birds
It sings praises to God almighty with its roar

Row upon row
Its waves roll in
With strength and majesty
It declares His presence
And His beauty

# ETCETERA

More poems to ponder!

# ACTION

Do you know that in each service
You can see the Word in action?

When people give their tithes,
There are the rich and poor,
When people give hugs and smiles,
That's God's love shinning

When praises and singing
About our Savior are given,
That's gratitude and glory
To God, our King

When people hold back, waiting for others
There are those who step out for Jesus
To do His will

Each action given in the name of the Lord
Is a blessing to Him
Why wait? Step out for Him
And bless Him this day

# ANTS

Everyone runs here and there
Like a giant ant pile
Each one to their own way,
Doing their own business

Their hearts are hardened
Do they fear the Lord?
No, for they do not recognize
That He lives

Please, Lord, we ask
To know the fear of the Lord
How awesome and majestic
You truly are

Don't let our hearts become hard
Soften us to Your Spirit's call
Teach us, show us the
Paths we must tread

For You are the God Almighty
And there is none other
We desire to see Your face
And be in Your presence
For only then will we be satisfied

# AWAITING

Christ, Emmanuel
Holy God, King of kings, Lord of lords
Righteous, Merciful, and Loving
Is He
Savior to all
Totally all in all

Into this world He came
Not as a king but as a
Child
Arrived in a manger
Righteous and true
Now He sits at the Father's side
Anticipating your arrival
To the New Jerusalem
Eternally loving you

# BANKING

Have you ever heard the song
"Soon and very soon
We are going to see the Lord"
Well, you can bank on it

For if the Lord tarries
And the rapture is put on hold
You definitely will meet the Lord
By death, face to face
When it is your time to go

There is still another way to meet Him
Here and now
Read and study His word
For it is all about Him
With much mercy, love, and hope for us

For He does not want one person to perish
And be away from Him
For eternity is forever
And Jesus has big plans
For you and me

# BEULAH

Beulah they call it
Married to the Lord
Drawing us to the land beautiful
Once again forevermore

No more tears
No more fears
Jesus the Christ is there
To be our Lord and true King

Unimaginable love and joy abound
Reunions with love ones are to be found
To see Jesus's face
And for Him to say, "Well done, good and faithful servant,
Welcome home"

# BLESSED

How blessed were they who saw the Lord
Who walked with Him day by day
Who heard His voice and felt His presence
How blessed were they

For today, we, too, can walk with the Lord
And be in His presence
To hear His voice
And go in His way
For we too are blessed day by day

# BREAK

Break the doom and gloom
Break the doom and gloom
Father God
Let your Son shine

Fill the places of despair
Bring the people out
Into the radiant light

Help them this day
To put them in your way

Break the despair
Cry hope—hope
To all
In the streets, homes, businesses
And back ways.

For such a time as this
New creations—all
For the time has come
To break the despair

# BUY

Saw a sign today
"Buy now, pay later"
Isn't it like
Sin now and pay later?

People don't think later will come
We all need to think of later
For it surely does come
And there be no hiding then

Turn now, this day
To the Lord God Almighty
Jesus the Christ is His name
He is the only way
For He did pay now
For your later

# CELEBRATE

Shimmering lights hang from roofs
Angelic faces peek from behind the shrubbery
Santa's, sleighs, and snowmen adorn front yards
Soon to come, a celebration

Food aplenty and gifts galore
To give to family and friends
How soon we forget
The reason for this season

This is the time to think of our Creator
Who came as a babe from heaven above
And graced us with His life and love

So, this Christmas time
Please consider Jesus the Christ
Who came to give His life for us
Celebrate, celebrate Him!

# COMING SOON

Be founded on the narrow way
The Rock that withstands all
Read the word each and everyday
For foundations strong and tall

Jesus Christ is the Way, the Truth, and Life
For soon, He will be coming for His wife
The bride of believers tried and true
Does that include you?

Be not deceived or deny
That the Son of God exists
For the day comes soon
When we all will kneel and bow
To the Great I Am

# COMPLETE

Men are men, and women are women
That's how we were designed
And through the grace of God, we meet
Not separate but joined
Only God can make this miracle complete

With God, all things are possible
That's why He needs to be within the two
So that His Spirit of love, power
And strength does shine through

# CRACKLE

Have you ever smelled the air during a thunder storm?
The earth gives off its fragrance
And soon, the air is crisp and clean

The earth is refreshed and renewed
It's like God's word
Really knowing Him and His heart's desire

So, spend time in His word
Desire His presence
First thing in the morning
So both you and He will face the day together

# CRYSTAL CLEAR

A baby is born
A child is nurtured
Soon to become a woman
Born of the Spirit

Married to one man
Mother of many
Devoted friend
True worshipper of God

Teacher of children
Helper to all
Joy flowing to others
Laughter erupting

Dancer of the Most High God
Strong love spanning generations
All found in this woman
Who loves the King of kings

# CRYSTALS

Like crystals that are pure and white
And snowflakes that are unique and light,
We should be to our Lord God, Jesus Christ

Each crystal has its own song
That's the way we are when we go before the throne
To be closer to Jesus Christ our God alone

So come this day, asking all rightly, to be before his presence
So you, too, can become all you were meant to be
Where the crystals are born

# DOORKEEPERS

Being a doorkeeper in the Kingdom
Is not a lowly task
For they welcome the children of the Most High
Keep out the sinners
Letting in only God's best

There is much responsibility
In keeping oneself clean
For there shall be no spot or wrinkle
On the Bride of the King

To do the Father's will
Keep yourself from the world
All its "pleasures" corrupted by man's ills

Keep yourself apart
Entangled you should not be
For soon enough
The royal King we shall see

# EWE

Ewe speak
Ewe speak the words of God
Ewe tell the people of His
Mighty works
Ewe speak of His love

The words roll from your mouth
As the ripples and waves on the water
They are not stopped by
Mere wood and stone
But go through on and out

For ewe speak the
Words of God
True and clear
No hidden word but truth
Plain and simple
As His word is

Give the people ears to hear, Lord
And a heart to desire You
So those ripples and waves of Your word
Are not hindered
But planted in fertile soil of the heart

# EXAMINATIONS

Perhaps you cried out to the Lord,
Change my heart
So others will desire my Jesus

Perhaps you've cried out,
Change them O Lord
For they are so wicked

Wicked they may be
But what of you
Has self deception gotten hold
Of your eye sight and heart

Examine yourself to know
If you be true before God
Before you cry out for others
Try your heart

For the Lord God Almighty
Sees the heart of all
So He is not fooled

Mercy and grace He gives
Anew each day
So we can come to the Father
Heart in hand
To Be His child

# EYE OPENER

To be a Christian is a very hard thing
For that is to be Christ-like
To have a heart filled with love
And with the right motives
For He died for billions of people
That denies Him, even today

When you give your heart and life to the Son of God
Your journey begins
Not through a "rose garden"
But through life with its tragedies and joys

They are all intertwined
To give you perseverance and character
To know who saved you
And in the end, to make you more and more like Christ

# FI-URE

That's right fi-Ure
Not fire
Call upon the Holy Spirit
He is the power
The comforter
Fi-Ure
Reign down upon me

Fi-Ure
Be with me Holy Spirit
Ablaze with your presence
To guide and teach
To do your will
Fi-Ure

# FOREVER

There's a song to be sung
To the Spirit
The Holy Spirit of God
Come, come be with us
Never to depart

Teach us what we should know
And plant it in our hearts
Not to stray from You
Ever, ever again

# FRESH

A new year has started
Fresh with many possibilities
Leave your old expectations behind
And begin to praise the Lord

Give Him the honor
And the respect due Him
To Him alone is all the glory
For He has done great things

From the breath in your body
To the sun in the sky
He has made everything
And it is very good

Thank Him and
Praise Him each day
For hope to rise up in you
And keep the enemy at bay

# FRUITFUL

One sings beautifully
Another works hard for their family
One gives marvelous hugs
Another spreads laughter

One is compassionate
Another listens and gives godly advice
One speaks the word of truth
Another points the way to Jesus Christ

Whether you are one or the other
Walk in the way
That the Lord God has given you
Be fruitful

# GIFTS

Bring a gift to the altar of God
Bring it this day
Whether it be tears or laughter
Still come to Him in each way

For He does not grow weary
Or faint in this world
He is the master of our walk
So indeed we may follow Him
Confident in His plans today

For He is faithful
Never ending in His love for us
So we too can be where He is
Loving Him as He loves us

# GIVING

Lord, You amaze me
That You would favor me
With Your mercy and grace

Each morning they are new
And in abundance
Holy, holy, holy are you

You give so much to each one of us
Grace, mercy, and love
Our hope is in you

You have sacrificed Your Son, Jesus
So that one day we will see You
Face-to-face, hearing your voice
No longer to be separated from You

# GOD'S MERCY

Whether you are on the top
Or whether you are on the bottom,
Whether you are loving and kind
Or whether you are hard or bitter,
We all need God's mercy

For you see, God's mercy
Is His love,
Which is unfathomable, unimaginable
By my hearts mind

When you misspeak
And hold hardness and/or bitterness
Toward people,
This is what you have in your
Heart toward God
No matter how much you tell
Yourself you love him

Call out, cry out,
Don't give up
On His mercy
For then you will have
God's love

# GOO GONE!

Isn't it better to be formed by God?
His breath within you, then to be a piece
Of galactic goo

To be a son or daughter of the King of
The universes
For a purpose of the Most High
To have value and life to follow

So come this day
And seek to know
That Jesus Christ is the one
To give you life eternally
In the days to come

# GRACE

There are times
When the Father
Gives you honor

You don't deserve it
It's nothing you've done
Sure sounds like grace to me

That's what we received
From Jesus
When He died upon the tree
Grace, grace, beautiful grace

# HELPING HANDS

White, brown, black, red, yellow
Hands made by God
For his service
Used by him
To give blessing help and love

Quiet hands
Busy hands
Healing hands from God

Your hands
Mine hands
Loving hands
Always from God

# LAYERS

Consider the rose
The deep, deep red rose
Its beauty is awesome
Its shape is divine

Yes, God created it
Just like you and me
Uniqueness in both
Yet the rose has unity
As the petals intertwine

Petal upon petal they
Provide relationship to each other
Like parent to children
And God with us
Side by side so close to be one

What wonderful creations
By God's design
To nurture, protect, and
Serve yours and mine

# LISTEN

Silence is golden so we have been told
Hearing is appropriate for us to be bold

Listen for the small voice within your heart
For God has been talking to you from the start

Can you hear what God is saying?
Will you listen with your being?

He sacrificed his blood for you
So the Father we would be seeing

Why do we matter to God the Father,
To his Son and the Holy Spirit?
The question has been asked

The answer is soon coming
It's Jesus unfathomable, unimaginable, and loving

# MORE ABUNDANTLY

True love and peace
Joy and laughter and trust

Air to breathe, food to eat
Health for your body
Abilities to walk and talk and think

Family and friends
Work to do
Talents of arts
To behold

All this and more
Comes from the Father of Lights
The Lord God strong and mighty
The Giver of Life
Jesus Christ
The soon coming King

# MOVING

Please, Lord, send the rain
A gentle rain
A soaking rain
For our land is dry and thirsty

Our spirits and bodies faint
For there is no water
Give us hope that You
Will once again revive us

Move us with Your Holy Spirit
O Holy One
To once again give You honor and glory
For Your names sake

# MY SON, MY DAUGHTER

I have seen the hard struggles
That you are going through
You are not alone, I am with you

I will not forget you or leave you
I love you much that it cannot be
Held by the sky or any other boundary

Your enemies don't have a chance
For I am with you
Just call to me when the waters come in
For I am with you

I know you, for your are written on the
Palms of my hands
I will be kind to you for you are
Precious to me
I love you with an everlasting love

Abba Father

# OIL OF FRAGRANCE

Sweet-smelling perfume
Couldn't be better
When you go through trials
For then you are the fragrance
To the Lord

High and higher the sweet
Smell ascends
To the Father
When you have gone through
Your trials

Don't give up
There's plenty of fragrance
To be had

One is peace
The deep down kind
Another is strength
To keep on keeping on
The other is love
For those around you

But most of all it's for the Father
Who loves you

# ON AND ON

Love doesn't stop with one person
It goes on and on and on
To be shared by others

Look what the Son of God did for all of us
Yes, for all
He gave His all, His life

So shouldn't we give our all to the Christ,
Who died for us,
So we can live with Him forever and ever?

# PARENTS

Parents, be careful of how you treat your children
Give them direction for the paths in their lives
Give them comfort when they are overwhelmed

Listen to them
Of their cares and worries
Of their ambitions
Do not stifle their talents
Be an encouragement to them

But most of all show them Jesus
How He loves them
And show how you love them too!
For to be a parent means
Sacrifice as Jesus did for us

# PRAY

Pray, pray for the mothers, fathers
And children too!
All of your relatives, friends
And acquaintances
And don't forget you

The needs are many
As the grains of sand
Large or small, take a stand
Ask the Father for His helping hand
To bring everyone to know
Jesus Christ, His Son

# RED SKIES

God's warnings are many
As He gave to the Hebrews
The waters were tainted
The frogs and flies abounded
Soon famine came to the land
Do you see the signs a coming?

God's people who are sleeping
Must awaken and turn back to Him
Not only for their sakes but
For those they love
For the day of wrath is closer
And soon the time of God's favor will be gone

Ask for boldness to speak of Him
Humble yourself before the Lord
For He will guide you
And give you words of hope for others

# RENOVATIONS

Rule in my heart and spirit this day, O Lord
Eternally to be at Your side
Never to be parted from You
Only to do Your pleasure
About Your business

Today, tomorrow, and all my days to come
Instead of my will, all for You, O Lord
Others to be drawn to You
Never to be parted
Salvation to be granted, safe and sure

# RESOLUTIONS

Here is something that is near and dear
To everyone here
New Year's resolutions
Are they really the solution?

Promise yourself to do better
Focus on God, treat others with kindness,
Excel in your life and/or lose weight
Aren't these 'promises' just fetters?

Change is what we want
Change is what we need
To keep our focus on Jesus Christ
So others will be drawn to Jesus' fire

# RISE 'N' SHINE

It is a good thing
To wake up with praises
For the King
Early in the morning, and late at night
To keep Jesus in your sight

So rise 'n' shine
With His praise on your lips
For the Holy Spirit will lead
You with His glorious tips
Throughout the day
In every way

# SIDE BY SIDE

Walk with the Lord
Side by side
Each and every day
Seeking His face
To see Him eye to eye

Follow His plan
For your life
To give Him pleasure
And finally to become His wife

Walk with the Lord
Side by side
Eternally blessed
For God is the best!
Walk, walk with the Lord

# SING

Sing to the Lord with your whole being
Speak words of encouragement to others
From your heart
Take the first step in friendships
For your God is with you from the start

He guides and directs your foot steps
He gives you wisdom and grace
For the Lord god sees you
And loves you with His whole heart

# SINGING SOLDIER

Sing to the Lord a new song
So His word does say
Sing the words of victory
For now and each day

Dress yourself in His word
So you may be heard
Marching to His beat
Quickly with your feet

Be a singing soldier
Follow Him each day
Conform to His wishes
And you'll be in His way

# SOON

In the darkness, He is there
Comforting, leading you quietly
To do His will
For His will is the best for you

Knowledge of the future has He
It is all in his hands
For the plans He has are
Good and not for harm

Trust in Him
Follow Him with all your heart
And the day comes soon
When we will see the
True Jesus Christ
Lover of all mankind

# STABILITY ABILITY

To have ability
Proven through and through

We must be tested
For stability to shine through

Ability is given by the Lord
Gifting us with talents to use

Stability is also from the Lord
Testing our hearts and courage not to lose

So, walk this day, hand in hand with the Lord
For both stability and ability to be proven in you

# STAY

To wait on the Lord is a very good thing
For He renews your strength, peace, and love
Trusting Him is the only way to go
For the world and its problems are too big

For He is our light, shield, and rock
In times of trouble and peace
So stay in His presence
And He truly will direct your ways

# STICKERS

People put stickers on other people
They may have been hurt by them
Perhaps they don't like them
Or they believe the stickers are true

If you have been "stickered"
And you don't know the reason,
Take it to the Lord
Lay it all at His feet

Ask of Him to search your heart
To make sure the stickers don't belong
Then leave the sticker behind
And walk in His love toward others

# STONE COLD

Many times the words "I forgive you" are spoken
But the heart is stone cold
No actions of forgiveness are given

Yet, by God's mercy and grace
Those words start a change so profound
That the heart is turned to flesh

A healing abounds to that heart
And passes on to others
Where soon the light of God
Shines forth, bringing love, peace, joy, and
True forgiveness

All this can be
Just let God into your heart

# SWEETNESS

There are some children that are contrary
Yet there are others that cooperate
With each other
And it is as sweetness to the soul

To dwell in unity is a beautiful thing
For God's love shines and shines
We should be like the children
Living in harmony
So we too, can be sweetness
To the Lord

# TAKE HEED

Take heed
Take heed
The end is near
Jesus is coming
Can't you hear?

Many will be offended
Betrayed by some
Murdered, imprisoned
Deceived by one

Endure to the end
My faithful one
For I am
The soon coming King

# THANK YOU

O Lord, You do sing over me
Of wonders and beauties
Please help me to see
Your hands on my life
Your heart toward me

Your songs of protection and wisdom
Are continually there
From the bottom of my soles
To the top of my hair

Thank You, dear Lord
For your mercies galore
Your love is overflowing
Encouraging, encompassing
And I am everlasting in Your care

# THE BLOOD

The blood of Jesus is not
Weak or transparent
Or can even fade away

The blood is strong and mighty
That saves and protects
And comes against the enemy

Ask the Lord to apply
His blood on you today
To be his in every way

For the blood of Jesus
Was at a high price
Our Savior gave willing for us

Now be totally His
Consumed by the blood
To be His very only

# THE CHALLENGE

Three boxes there are
In the center, one is golden
Beautiful beyond compare
Engraved with filigree gold

The second one
Is jade in color
Precious and delicate in stature
Steady and sure

The last is common-looking
Functional you might say
Different shades of brown and gray
Meld across its surface

So, which has the most value?
Is just one or the other
Or is it all three
Three in one
Who do you see?

# THE COSTING

To count the cost
And say not my will
But, Yours O Lord
Is a very hard thing
For the flesh wages war
Mightily for you

So decisions to turn from the flesh
Will change the future
Not only yours but those You love
So they too can follow the Most High God

So truly, flesh must die
For life to begin with God

# THE HOLE

When the four men lowered their paralyzed friend
Down the hole in the roof
Jesus looked up and saw their faith
He told the man his sins were forgiven
To take up his mat and go home

Well now ——

Can't you see the four men on the roof
Jumping, dancing and shouting 'round?

See, Levi, I told you he could do it
This Jesus of Nazareth
Is the great miracle worker
Samuel said

What of the man who walked out
Amazement and surprise covered him
For he thought he would not ever walk again
Then, he started to give praise to God
For his mighty miracle

# THE MISSION

The hand of the Lord God Almighty is upon us
For such a time as this
To bring His Word to the captives of this world
To give them hope
So they too, will know that He loves them dearly

You've heard these words before
Now pray to the Father to do His will
To help those in trouble and bound in chains

How you may ask
Speak words of life
Lend a listening ear
A helping hand, or a hug or two
And maybe some tears too

For it is only through Jesus Christ
Who is the way, the truth, and the life
That they will be saved from the darkness to come

# THE ROBE

Diaphanous in appearance
But solid through and through
Is the robe of glory

Full of glittering gems and solid gold
The tears of the saints
Are upon and in it too

Filled with smoke and fire
Length unimaginable
Encompassing all the universes

This is the robe of glory
God's sacrificial love for you

# THOUGHTS

Thoughts come and go
Some are good
And some are not so much

We are to think on things
That are true, pure, right
Holy, friendly, and proper

Thoughts that matter
And are worthy of praise
For God Almighty knows everything
In where your heart lays

# THREE

Fire, wind, and the rain
Are all used by God the Father
To bring you closer to him

Fire, the desire to know Him
Wind, to move you
And the rain to bless and
Grow you in His ways

Much is done by the fire
It purifies you
Sears your sins and
Cleans the rooms of your heart

The wind is steady and sure,
Giving direction and
Wisdom to live your life
And move in His ways

Then comes the rain
The healing rain
To grow you in abundance
By reaching out to others
To speak of His loving ways

So then, the fire, the wind
And the rain
Are God's ways
For you to know Him

# TIMES

The times of the holidays are upon us
Visiting and feasting abound
People are exchanging gifts
Food and merriment are certainly around

Celebrate with those that have no one
Include them in your joy
Take time to visit with Jesus Christ
For He is truly the reason for this season

# TIMING

When the Son of God came to earth,
It was the right time
There was no machinery
And technology
To cloud men's minds

From age to age
Men and women are the same
Looking to themselves
Their hearts are far from God
Thinking they are *self-sufficient*

Testings and problems come
At the exact right time
To show God's presence and love
That He is not far away
But He *is* God with us

# TOMORROW

Do not fret
Do not worry
Heaven's waiting
For those who love Jesus

For you see, our eyes
And mind
Can't see or conceive of what
Heaven is like

But we will have our
Own place
That He has chosen
For Jesus has promised this for us

Then out and about
To do His bidding
Eternally satisfied with
His will for us
Doing His pleasure
And living for Him

# TREMORS

Do not tremble
Do not fear
For the Lord Jesus Christ
Is very near

He will take you through the dark times
Lift you up and secure your place
Just concentrate
And look into His face

# VEILS

Not the sheerest of veils
To keep us apart, dear Lord
Not the thinnest of smoke
To hide me away from You

Know me this day
All of me
The deepest recesses of my heart
Make me true for You

Help me to be obedient to Your word
Not going to the left or right
But straight with You

Direct my steps in the way I should go
Listening with my heart and spirit
As You will me to know

Let this day unfold
As You have seen long ago
Your will I ask for now and forever
For the way I should go

# WAY

Relationships are made in heaven
But forged on this earth
Love, mercy, and grace
Are given to the Lord's delight

Forgiveness and long suffering,
Peace and joy
Are given by the Spirit
Isn't this just right?

Words may fail
And actions may go astray
But keep going back to the Spirit
For Him to have His way

# WHISPERS

Whisper sweet some things to the Lord this day
Tell Him of your love for His way
The sacrifices He made for you and me
So we, too, can be on the way

Throughout the day
Remember to say
I love You, Lord
And thank you for this day

# WINDS

New winds of change
Are over us
To revive, restore, and
Rearm you

Anticipate, long for
The new winds
For the Father gives abundantly
To those who ask

Ask for them to blow over you
To clean, guide, and protect you

For what was once lost
Or hidden
Can be used by God

When you truly desire
The new winds of change

# WINNERS

Does anyone hear?
Does anyone care?
How far the people have fallen
Fallen, fallen, fallen from grace
To hit bottom
And the Lord God Almighty's face

They have turned to their insanity
Made sin right and virtue wrong
So they have done
Judgment is soon to come

For they truly don't know
What they have done
But the tragedy is
They don't care
For they think they have won

Please, dear Lord, have mercy

# YO!

Do you feel like a yo-yo?
Do you go up and down
And sideways too?

Don't fret
Don't look any longer
The answer to keep you straight
Is Jesus of Nazareth

He's the one who died to save you
He's the one to take the yo-yoing away
For He's the rock to steady you
So seek Him today

Then you too will have a purpose
Your road will be sure
Come, come this day to Jesus
So you will be a yo-yo no more

# YOKES

None of God's children will be ashamed
When they wait upon Him
For His paths are filled with grace and mercy

Give Him the hard yokes upon your shoulders
The situations that seem to have no remedy
But for God
These will vanish in His time
Leaving you stronger and with wisdom

So come this day
And leave your burdens behind
With the God who loves you